The Finance Explorer

A Kids Book Exploring the Basics of Starting a Business and Investing!

Book 2 of the My First Finance Illustrated Book Series

Written by Ben Hofstetter and Nick Zehrung

New Caney, TX
2023

A book in the Children's Financial Literacy and Learning Path

Library of Congress Control Number: 2023918047

Table of Contents

"Today I will do what others won't, so tomorrow I can do what others can't."

- Jerry Rice

Chapter 1:

The Lemonade Stand Adventure:

Learning About Business and Helping Others

For Parents

Key Themes Explored in this chapter:

- Providing value to the community can generate income, as shown through the establishment of a lemonade stand.

- The basics of investing in your own small business, as shown through using money earned by doing chores to fund the start-up costs of a lemonade stand.

- Showing the basics of setting up a small community business by walking through the steps of setting up a lemonade stand.

- Learning the difference between a personal budget and a financial statement for a business, where the goal of a budget is to be at $0 and the business should make a profit.

In the first book we talked about what money is, and how we make it. We showed that by bringing value to the people around us, good things might happen.

In this book, we'll show that this idea can get expanded to our whole community, not just the people we know!

For example, lemonade stands are a great way to provide something cold for your neighbors to drink on a hot summer's day! We'll continue to build on this example throughout the chapter!

If we want to make a lemonade stand and bring some value to our community, then the first step is to buy the supplies to make lemonade! We can use the money we earned from doing chores for our family and friends to buy the supplies!

It's called an investment when we use our hard-earned money to start a business that makes our community better! In this case we're investing our money into a lemonade stand that many people will enjoy!

The next step in setting up the lemonade stand is to actually make some lemonade! We'll use lemons, sugar, and water to make a yummy drink that we can try before sharing with our community!

No matter what service you are providing to your community, you want to make sure it's good quality before selling it! Maybe your first batch of lemonade isn't perfect, but by the second or third time you will have mixed the ingredients in an amazing way!

The next step is to let people know about your lemonade stand! You can create colorful posters and flyers to advertise your stand in your neighborhood and other local businesses like a coffee shop (if you ask permission)!

This is a concept called advertising, and it's how you find customers to buy your lemonade!

A good advertisement lets people know what you're selling, where you'll be, when you'll be there, and how much it will cost!

Now it's time to set up your stand! For a lemonade stand you'll want a busy area that people walk by all the time so they can see your stand. You want to at least have a table, cups, and a pitcher of lemonade. Don't forget to put up a sign with the price and what you're selling!

Picking a good location and having all the supplies ready is very important for the success of the lemonade stand! Choosing an area that people don't travel by means that they won't see your stand. Or if you don't come prepared with the right supplies, you might not be able to serve the number of people that want to buy lemonade!

Now that you're open for business it's time to greet your customers! You should treat all of your customers like they are your best friend and be polite to everyone that stops by!

Remember, the secret to selling a lot of lemonade is being a genuinely nice person! Nobody wants to buy things from mean people, so be nice and watch your sales soar!

As customers buy your lemonade, make sure to keep track of how much money you're making! This is important for understanding the income on the Financial Statement for your lemonade stand!

A Financial Statement for a small business is very similar to the Budget that we learned about in Book 1!

On the next page we'll show what a Financial Statement looks like and the differences between it and a Budget!

Remember that the goal of our personal budget is to equal $0, so that we always know where our money is going. Our personal budget was made up of three categories.

$$\begin{array}{l} \quad \text{Income} \\ - \text{Expenses} \\ - \text{Investments} \\ \hline = 0 \end{array}$$

The goal of a Financial Statement isn't to have $0 remaining, it's to have a positive number left over, which is called a Profit! Making a profit means you've made more money than it cost to run the business! Profits then get converted into personal income on your Budget, just like above!

$$\begin{array}{l} \quad \text{Business Income} \\ - \text{Business Expenses} \\ - \text{Re-investments} \\ \hline = \text{Profits} \end{array}$$

Let's show this in a quick example.

We'll start by investing $10 to buy the supplies for our stand. This investment counts as business income because it's money brought into the lemonade stand.

On a busy Saturday we made $40, and on Sunday we made $20! Our customers loved the lemonade in the first weekend!

We had a $10 expense to buy the supplies for Saturday, and then a $15 expense to restock our supplies for Sunday since we sold so much on Saturday.

We didn't make any re-investments over this first weekend. An example of a re-investment would be if we bought a better table for our lemonade stand.

With these numbers in mind, our simple Financial Statement would look like this for the opening weekend of our lemonade stand!

	$70	Business Income ($10 + $40 + $20)
–	$25	Business Expenses ($10 + $15)
–	$0	Re-investments
=	$45	Profits

Now that you have figured out how much Profit you've made it's time to figure out what to do with it!

One option is to pay it all to yourself for your hard work! Another option is to re-invest into the business. On the previous page we didn't show this, but sometimes it's a good idea! Buying better supplies can make your business stand out from others and keep customers coming back to buy from you!

Maybe you could buy items to add a fun Pirate theme to your lemonade stand so that your customers remember you?

As you gain experience you might start to think of other ways to provide benefit and value to your community! Maybe you can mow your neighbors lawn, or start a car wash!

Once you learn how to provide value to your community the possibilities become endless!

"If you want to go fast, go alone. If you want to go far, go together"

- African Proverb

Chapter 2:

The Lawn Mowing Adventure:

Investing in Your Friend's Business

For Parents

Key Themes Explored in this chapter:

- This chapter explores the basics of investing in a business, by walking through investing in a friends lawn mowing business.
- Discover the significance of conducting research before making any investment, with suggested questions to ask your friend about their lawn care business.
- Understand the fundamentals of structuring a loan agreement, including the amount lent, repayment terms, and the due date.
- Learn about the distinction between fixed returns and interest-based returns, along with a simplified explanation of what interest rates are.

Bringing value to your community can take many forms. In this chapter we'll explore supporting your friends and neighbors by investing in their businesses!

Imagine your friend wants to start a lawn mowing business. It costs a lot of money to buy a lawn mower and the gas to make it work. You can be a great friend and make a smart business choice by investing in your friend's business. This means you're helping them with the costs and expecting them to pay you back.

It's different from just letting your friend borrow some money or giving them money for small things. Investing in our friends means actively supporting their dreams while also being responsible with money.

Investing in our friend's business is a very serious matter. Always remember to discuss with your Parent or Guardian before making a decision with your money!

Investing in a friend's business is different from running your own lemonade stand. You can make money without doing the work yourself. Your friend runs the business, and you get a portion of the profit.

Remember in the last chapter, we invested $10 into our lemonade stand, bought supplies, and did all the work. We made $45 in profit, which was great!

When you invest in your friend's business, you give them the $10, but they do all the work. However, instead of making $45, your friend gives you $15 ($10 + $5), and your friend keeps $30. We'll learn more about this as we continue through the chapter!

Before investing your money, discuss with your friend how they will use it for their business. Make sure they have a clear plan for making their lawn mowing business successful!

Check if their business idea makes sense and will generate more money. Remember what we learned in Book 1, providing value to the community is how we make money. If their idea doesn't seem like it will add value to the people around them, it might not be a good investment!

Before you invest you also need to create an agreement with your friend that clearly shows how much money you are investing, how much money you expect in return, and when you expect to have your money back by!

Establishing these three simple things before you give someone money can save you a lot of problems in the future!

When your friend's business earns money, they should give you back the money you invested and the agreed-upon extra amount.

In the next few pages, we'll explore the concept of Interest as a way to repay money. It's commonly used by adults, so it's important to learn about it now.

When you're young, sometimes it's easier to agree on a specific amount. Here's an example: "I'll invest $20 with you now, and in one month, you'll give me $25 back." Notice how this agreement has the three main elements: how much is invested, when it's due back by, and how much is due.

This type of agreement is probably the best for most situations between friends!

Another way you can agree to be paid back is through Interest. Interest is like a special thank you gift for lending your money, where your friend pays you a little extra on top of the amount you invested.

The easiest way to think of an interest rate is as a number which shows how risky an investment is. So the more risk involved in an investment, the higher the interest rate will be, which means more money will need to be repaid.

Risk in an investment is determined by many factors, but there's some common sense ways to think of it. For instance, if your friend live in an apartment complex and doesn't have any neighbors with a lawn, it would be pretty risky to start a lawn mowing business!

We'll go through this with numbers on the next page!

Let's say you invest $10 into your friends business, and they agree to pay you back at a 10% interest rate for every month they have your $10. This means, that every month, they owe you $1 more. So if your friend keeps your money for 6 months, they would owe you $16 back. The original $10 + $6 in interest!

In the adult world, interest rates are calculated over the course of a year, but for the ease of learning we used a month!

Remember, when you invest in your friends business the goal isn't to make as much money as possible. The goal is to provide value to your friend by giving them the money they need to get their business going. And then you both win by making money together!

Investing in your friend's business can inspire you to think of other ways to provide value to your community!

When you see your friend's lawn mowing business doing really well, it should make you feel happy and proud. You should feel great knowing that you helped them succeed by giving them the money they needed to start their business!

"The more you learn, the more you earn."

- Warren Buffett

Chapter 3:

The Lemonade Fund:

Unlocking the Magic of Mutual Funds for Young Investors

For Parents

Key Themes Explored in this chapter:

- This chapter explores the fundamentals of stock market investing by discussing mutual funds (as a stand in for all collective investment funds).
- Gain an understanding of mutual funds and indexes through a relatable example of a class of kids investing together in multiple lemonade stands, with their teacher as the fund manager.
- Discover the lower risk associated with collective fund investing compared to individual stock investing, using the performance of lemonade stands within the mutual fund as an illustration.
- Emphasize the importance of patience and resilience in market investing, highlighting the long-term outlook as a more powerful position than short-term gains or losses.

In the last chapter we discussed investing in one small business that was started by someone we know, our friend!

In this chapter we're going to discuss a different way of investing. With this method, we combine our money with other people and invest in many big businesses!

You may have heard the term "the stock market" before! In this chapter were going to use a small example to show what happens when you invest in the stock market!

Just remember, before you make any decisions with your money to ask your parent or guardian to make sure it's a good idea!

The safest and easiest way to invest in the stock market is by investing with other people. This is often called a "mutual fund."

To explain what a mutual fund is, let's start by imagining your school and three kids who have their own lemonade stands.

As you grow older, you'll come across other names like Indexes or Exchange-Traded Funds for groups of people investing together. In this book, we'll stick to using the term mutual fund to explain the concept. Future advanced learner books will cover the differences in more detail!

Next, let's imagine that your school class has 20 students and 1 teacher.

One day, your class decides to invest together. So all the students bring in $5 and give it to the teacher to invest for you.

Now your teacher has $100 to invest on behalf of the whole class!

Mutual funds always have someone or something that you give your money to when you invest! Often times in real life this looks like just numbers on a computer screen, but in the background there is a real group of people who are investing your money for you; just like your teacher in this example!

Your teacher wants to invest the class's $100 wisely. They decide to put different amounts of money into three lemonade stands based on how likely each stand is to succeed!

Here's how your teacher invests the classes $100:

a) Stand 1: $30
b) Stand 2: $50
c) Stand 3: $20

This is where investing in a mutual fund gets exciting! Instead of investing in just one business, when you pool your money with others, you can invest in multiple businesses at once!

Your teacher can give you updates on the lemonade stands whenever you want, but with mutual funds it's better not to check them every day. In this example you and your teacher decide to get updates once a week.

In real life, it's not the best idea to invest in mutual funds for short time periods. Instead, we should try to invest a little bit of money on a consistent basis and let it grow for a long time! We'll see why later in the chapter!

After a month, your teacher says the class's investment is now worth $120! They also tell you the value of each lemonade stand.

You might see that two stands went down in value while one went up. It may seem confusing, but we'll explain how this works on the next page!

a) Stand 1: $25
b) Stand 2: $40
c) Stand 3: $55

The great thing about mutual funds is that we invested in more than one lemonade stand - we invested in three! In real life, mutual funds invest in lots of different companies. The most common one invests in the top 500 companies in the United States!

At the beginning of the chapter we said that mutual funds are one of the safest ways to invest in the stock market. This example shows why!

If you had invested in just one lemonade stand, you might have chosen one that lost money. But by investing in a mutual fund with your class, your money was spread across all three stands. The profit from one stand made up for the losses of the other two!

You may be curious why two stands lost money while one stand made more. We'll provide a simple example on the next page to help you understand. Remember, this happens in the real world too!

Sometimes things happen that affect how much profit a business makes.

In this example, let's assume that the two lemonade stands that lost money were on the west side of town, and the stand that made money was on the east side of town.

Unfortunately, the two stands on the west side of town didn't read the weather report and didn't know a storm was coming through. The other stand owner did see the storm was coming and decided to set up where it wasn't going to rain!

Because of the storm the people who lived on the west side of town didn't come out for lemonade, but the people on the east side of town bought lots of lemonade!

Storms can affect big businesses in real life just as much as they can affect lemonade stands! That's why it's important to invest in many businesses and not just one!

Now that we know the class mutual fund is worth $120 it's time to get our money back!

Remember that we had 20 students in our class and each student invested $5.

The teacher starts by giving each student their $5 back. Each student then gets $1 from the gains that the mutual fund made!

This means that each student made $1 without having to do any work at all! How awesome is that!?

In real life, it's best to keep your money in a mutual fund for a long time unless you really need it! Mutual funds give you the most money when you let the money grow over time. In the next book we'll show this by exploring the powers of compound interest!

Remember, all investments have risks. Sometimes the value goes down instead of up, and you might lose money in the short term. Don't worry if this happens!

On the next page we'll see why we shouldn't get scared when this happens, and we should leave our money invested!

Investing in mutual funds and making money works in waves! Historically, the value of a mutual fund will rise for a long time, and then lower for a little bit. But just like a wave, they have always started rising again, maybe one day they'll go as high as the moon!

You can see this in action now if you want! Ask a parent or guardian to use a search engine to look up the S&P 500. Set the time to Max and look at the waves over the last 40 years!

Thank you for reading Book 2 of the My First Finance Illustrated Book Series! We hope it generated some great ideas as you teach your children about the world of investing!

Look out for Book 3 of the series where we discuss bringing value to your community through philanthropy and education, as well as the power of long term investing!

If you enjoyed this book, we have a series of coloring books published titled the "My First Finance Coloring Book Series" which can be found on Amazon! The concepts follow the same pattern as this book, but are written for a younger audience. There are plenty of fun pictures to color, along with a few activities!

You can also follow us on Instagram for more great content and activities to try at home!

myfirstfinancebook

Reach out with questions to
www.myfirstfinancebook.com

www.ingramcontent.com/pod-product-compliance
Lightning Source LLC
LaVergne TN
LVHW071411210926
848486LV00004B/250
* 9 7 8 1 9 6 2 5 4 3 0 9 5 *